ELEPHANTASTIC.

KINGFISHER
Larousse Kingfisher Chambers Inc.
95 Madison Avenue
New York, New York 10016

First American edition 1995
2 4 6 8 10 9 7 5 3

LIBRARY OF CONGRESS CATALOGING-IN-PUBLICATION DATA
Hurt-Newton, Tania.
Elephantastic / Tania Hurt-Newton. — 1st American ed.
p. cm.
1. Elephants—Juvenile humor. 2. Wit and humor, Juvenile.
3. Riddles, Juvenile. I. Title.
PN6231.E5H87 1995
808.88'2—dc20 94-37194 CIP AC

ISBN 1-85697-569-X

Edited by Abigail Willis
Designed by Chris Fraser

Printed in Hong Kong

ELEPHANTASTIC!

A TRUNKFUL OF UNFORGETTABLE JOKES

illustrated by

TANIA HURT-NEWTON

Kingfisher

NEW YORK

Why do elephants want to be alone?
Because two's a crowd.

What's gray and moves at
a hundred miles an hour?
*A jet-propelled
elephant.*

What's big and gray and wears a mask?
The Elephantom of the Opera.

What's gray with red spots?
An elephant with the measles.

What's gray and never needs ironing?
A drip-dry elephant.

What's big and red and gray?
A sunburned elephant.

What's gray, stands in a river during a storm, and doesn't get wet?
An elephant with an umbrella.

What's gray and goes around and around?
An elephant in a washing machine.

What's gray and powdery?
Instant elephant mix.

What's gray and
highly dangerous?
*An elephant with a
machine gun.*

What's big and gray and lives in Scotland?
The Loch Ness Elephant.

What's yellow on the outside and gray on the inside?

An elephant disguised as a banana.

What's big and gray and protects you from the rain?

An umbrellaphant.

What's gray, wrinkly, and has sixteen wheels?

An elephant on roller-skates.

What's big, gray, and flies straight up?
An elecopter.

What's gray, has four legs, and jumps up and down?
An elephant on a trampoline.

What's bright red and weighs four tons?
An elephant holding its breath.

What's blue and has big ears?
An elephant at the North Pole.

elephant enterprises

What's gray and wrinkly and jumps every twenty seconds?
An elephant with hiccups.

What goes up slowly but comes down fast?
An elephator.

restaurant / bar

stock room

What has three tails, seven feet, and four trunks?
An elephant with spare parts.

basement

What's as big as an elephant but weighs nothing?

An elephant's shadow.

What's gray and lights up?
An electric elephant.

What's gray but turns red?
An embarrassed elephant.

What's gray, carries a bunch of flowers, and cheers you up when you're sick?
A get-wellephant.

What's big and gray with horns?
An elephant marching band.

What's gray, has a wand, huge wings, and gives money to elephants?
The tusk fairy.

What's gray, beautiful, and wears glass slippers?
Cinderelephant.

What's the difference between an injured elephant and bad weather?
One roars with pain, the other pours with rain.

FRED: What's the difference between an elephant and a mailbox?
BERT: I don't know.
FRED: Well, I'm not sending you to mail my letters.

What's the difference between an elephant and a bad pupil?
One rarely bites, the other barely writes.

How do you tell the difference between a mouse and an elephant?
Try picking them up!

What's the difference between an elephant and a piece of paper?
You can't make a paper airplane out of an elephant.

What's the difference between a sick elephant and seven days?

One is a weak one, the other is one week.

What's the difference between an elephant and a banana?

Have you ever tried to peel an elephant?

What's the difference between an elephant and a strawberry?

A strawberry is red.

Why are elephants gray?
So you can tell them apart from flamingos.

What's the difference between an elephant and a flea?
An elephant can have fleas but a flea can't have elephants.

What's the difference between an African elephant and an Indian elephant?
About three thousand miles.

What's worse than an elephant with a
sore trunk?
A centipede with sore feet.

Why is an elephant large, gray, and wrinkled?
*Because if it were small, white, and round it
would be an aspirin.*

ELEPHANT KEEPER: "My elephant isn't
  well. Do you know a good animal doctor?"
ZOO KEEPER: "No, I'm afraid all the doctors
  I know are people."

PATIENT: Doctor, doctor, I keep seeing pink
  and yellow elephants.
DOCTOR: Have you seen a psychiatrist?
PATIENT: No, only pink and yellow elephants.

Why do elephants scratch themselves? *Because they're the only ones who know where they itch.*

ELEPHANT: "Doctor, I've lost my memory!"
DOCTOR: "When did this happen?"
ELEPHANT: "When did what happen?"

Why is a sneezing elephant like a spy?
They both have a code in the head.

What pills do you give an elephant that can't sleep?
Trunkquillizers.

A boy with an elephant on his head went to see a doctor. The doctor said, "You know, you really need help."

"*Yes I do*," the elephant cried, "*get this kid off my foot!*"

What kind of elephants live in Antarctica?
Cold ones.

Why do elephants have trunks?
Because they'd look silly carrying suitcases.

How do you get five elephants into a small car?
Two in the back, two in the front, and one in the glove compartment.

How does an elephant get out of a small car?
The same way he got in.

Why did the elephant cross the road?
Because the chicken was having a day off.

What do you call an elephant at the
North Pole?
Lost.

Which takes less time to get ready for a trip, an elephant or a rooster?
A rooster—he only takes his comb.

What did the hotel manager say to the elephant who couldn't pay her bill?
"Pack your trunk and clear out."

How do you get an elephant into a matchbox?
Take all the matches out first.

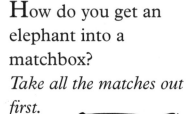

What happened to the elephant who ran
away with the circus?
The police made him bring it back!

Why shouldn't you take an elephant to a zoo?
Because she'd rather go to the movies.

How can you tell if an elephant has been in your fridge?
Footprints in the butter.

What did the grape say when the elephant stepped on it?
Nothing. It just let out a whine.

How do you know if there's an elephant in your dessert?
You get very lumpy ice cream!

"I know an elephant who lives on garlic alone."
"I'm not surprised he lives alone if all he eats is garlic."

Why are elephants wiser than chickens?
Ever heard of Kentucky Fried Elephant?

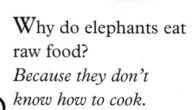

Why do elephants eat raw food?
Because they don't know how to cook.

Have you heard about the elephant who went on a crash diet?
He wrecked a bus, three cars, and a fire engine.

Why did the elephant eat candles?
For light refreshment.

What do you do with a green elephant?
Wait until it ripens.

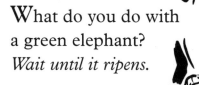

Why did the elephant sleep in a bowl of salad dressing?
So she'd wake up really oily.

What do invisible
elephants drink?
Evaporated milk.

When should you
feed elephant milk to
a baby?
*When it's a baby
elephant.*

If you were making an
omelette would you
choose chicken eggs or
elephant eggs?
*Chicken eggs because
elephant yolks are
usually terrible!*

An elephant walked into a cafe and ordered a strawberry milkshake. He drank it in one gulp, paid, and left.

The customers in the cafe couldn't believe their eyes. One of them said to the waitress, "What an amazing elephant! Has he done that before?"

"Oh, no," said the waitress. "Normally he has a small soda."

How do you know peanuts are fattening?
Have you ever seen a skinny elephant?

What do you call an elephant
who can't add?
Dumbo.

"My elephant plays chess with me."

"How amazing! It must be a really intelligent animal."

"Not really. I've won three games out of five so far today."

JIM: "My homework's really difficult tonight—
I have to write an essay on the elephant."
JOHN: "Well, for a start, you're going to need
a very big ladder..."

Why do elephants do well in school?
Because they have a lot of gray matter.

TEACHER: "To which family does the
elephant belong?"
PUPIL: "I don't know, nobody I know
owns one."

"How do you spell elephant?"

"E-l-l-e-e-f-a-n-t."

"That's not how the dictionary spells it."

"You didn't ask me how the dictionary spells it."

TEACHER: "Name six wild animals."

PUPIL: "Two lions and four elephants."

TEACHER: "Where would you find an elephant?"

PUPIL: "You don't have to find them— they're too big to lose."

Tarzan was tired when he came home.

"What have you been doing?" asked Jane.

"Chasing a herd of elephants on vines."

"Really?" said Jane. "I thought elephants stayed on the ground."

Why shouldn't you go into the jungle at noon?

Because that's when elephants practice parachuting.

=3=

What is an easy way to get a wild elephant?
Buy a tame one and annoy it.

What did Tarzan say when he saw the elephants coming? *"Here come the elephants!"*

What's the best way to see a charging herd of elephants? *On television!*

Why don't elephants like playing cards in the jungle? *Because of all the cheetahs.*

What do you call an elephant that never takes a bath?
A smellyphant.

What do you call an elephant with a carrot in each ear?
Anything, she can't hear you.

What do you call an elephant with a machine gun?
Sir!

What can an elephant with a machine gun call you?
Anything he likes!

What do you call an
elephant that's small
and pink?
A failure.

What do you call an elephant who lies across
the middle of a tennis court?
Annette!

30,40

What do you call an
elephant creeping
through the jungle
in the middle of
the night?
Russell!

What do you call an elephant with a seagull on its head?
Cliff!

What do you call an elephant with a rabbit up its sweater?
Warren!

What do you call the rabbit up the elephant's sweater?
Terrified!

What do you call someone with an elephant on their head?
Squashed.

How do elephants speak to each other?
By 'elephone.

What did the zookeeper say when he saw
three elephants in sunglasses coming over
a hill?
Nothing, he didn't recognize them.

When do elephants have eight feet?
When there are two of them.

How can you tell when there's an elephant under the bed?
When you're nearly touching the ceiling.

Z Z z

What do you give an
elephant with big feet?
Plenty of room.

What do you say when an elephant sits on
your sofa?
It's time to get a new sofa!

Why did the elephant walk on two legs?
To give the ants a chance.

Why do elephants have trunks?
Because they have no pockets to put things in.

A man was sprinkling white powder on his lawn.

"Why are you doing that?" asked his neighbor.

"It's to keep the elephants off the grass," he replied.

"But we don't get any elephants around here!"

"I know—good stuff, isn't it?"

Which animals were the last to leave the ark?
The elephants, because they had to pack their
trunks.

What would happen if an elephant sat in
front of you at the movies?
You would miss most of the film.

What steps would you take if you were being
chased by an elephant?
Big ones.

What do you find
in an elephants'
graveyard?
Elephantoms.

Why do elephants
have wrinkly ankles?
*Because their shoes are
too tight.*

Which is stronger, an
elephant or a snail?
*A snail, because it
carries its house. An
elephant only carries
its trunk.*

What do you do with
old cannon balls?
*Give them to elephants
to use as marbles.*

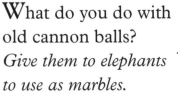

What do elephants
do in the evenings?
Watch 'elevision.

Who lost a herd of
elephants?
Big Bo Peep.

What is an elephant's
favorite film?
Elephantasia.

What do elephants
say as a compliment?
You look elephantastic!

What did the elephant
say to the famous
detective?
*It's ele-mentary, my
dear Sherlock.*

ZOOKEEPER: "I've lost one of my elephants."
OTHER ZOOKEEPER: "Why don't you put an
  advertisement in the paper?"
ZOOKEEPER: "Don't be silly, he can't read."

What do you do if you find a blue elephant?
Try to cheer it up.

Why did the elephant jump in the lake when it began to rain?
To stop getting wet.

What is a baby
elephant after she is
five weeks old?
Six weeks old.

What did the elephant say when the man
grabbed him by the tail?
This is the end of me.

POLICEMAN: "One of your elephants has been seen chasing someone on a bicycle."
ZOOKEEPER: "Nonsense. None of my elephants knows how to ride a bicycle."

Why are elephants wrinkled all over?
Because they don't fit on an ironing board.

What do you get if you cross a parrot with an elephant?
An animal that tells you everything it remembers.

What do elephants sing at Christmas?
No-elephants, No-elephants . . .

Who do elephants get their Christmas presents from?
Elephanta Claus!

How do you hire an elephant?
Stand it on four bricks.

"Dad! Mom is fighting with an enormous elephant in the front yard!"

"Don't worry, dear, I'm sure the elephant can look after itself."

"Hey! My elephant
has no trunk."
"How does he smell?"
"Terrible!"

How are elephants and
hippopotamuses alike?
Neither can play basketball.

How do you keep an angry elephant from charging?
Take away its credit cards.

What did the baby elephant get when the daddy elephant sneezed?
Out of the way!

Why do elephants have short tails?
They can't remember long stories.

How do you keep an
elephant in suspense?
I'll tell you tomorrow.

Why is an elephant braver than a hen?
Because the elephant isn't chicken.

What's worse than raining cats and dogs?
Raining elephants.

What should you do if an elephant breaks down your front door?
Escape through the back door.

How do you raise a baby elephant that has been abandoned by its parents?
With a fork-lift truck.

FATHER: "I'd like an elephant for my son, please."
PET STORE OWNER: "Sorry, sir, we don't do exchanges."

Why was the elephant wearing red shoes?
Because her black ones were at the cobblers.

Hey, wait up! Now the elephants have had their turn it's time for me to blow my horn. So, okay, maybe I don't have 40,000 muscles in my nose but I have a few good qualities all the same. For a start, I'm not ten feet tall and I don't weigh five tons, which is just as well, because it would make drawing pretty tricky. I'm a real animal lover, something you can't help if you've grown up in Africa like I have.

I started drawing when I was a kid and haven't stopped since. Now I live in London with two "wild" tabby cats and no elephants. I just hope there will still be some elephants left in the world if I ever feel like inviting one over....

Tania